when love cracks

Shelby L. LaLonde

A Collection of Poems and Prose

All Poems are original works by Shelby L. LaLonde © 2019

Edited by Sheila M. Moon
Book Cover Created by Island @ SelfPubBookCovers.com

When Love Cracks/ Shelby L. LaLonde. -- 1st ed.

ISBN: 978-1-7336785-0-6 ebook ISBN: 978-1-7336785-1-3

Library of Congress Control Number: 2019901524

For the sensitives.

Contents

A NOTE FROM YOUR STORYTELLER:

The question isn't is it true love or not, The question is whether or not you can be with a person and be a productive and fulfilled individual while coexisting within each- others world.

These works tell a story about one of the most serious injuries that a human being can acquire in a lifetime. A broken heart.

Being brokenhearted is a painful existence that hinges on purpose and acceptance. Understanding that love does not have a definable definition. We need experience and are drawn to the people that can bring us to our gifts, of which often times are born of our sorrows. Love is all-encompassing.

Learning to accept the things that twist and tear out our heart is still a mystery to most of us. Yet within that mystery lies our destiny and our power. You can hold onto your pain all you want, and most do, but that's not the way we were meant to live. At some point we need to reconcile the fact that we have the ability to save ourselves. Often it's heartbreak that delivers us that conclusion.

How do you get over love? You don't. There is no getting over love. It just gets transformed. Shapeshifts into something that brings us closer to ourselves.

These words were written at a time in my life where I discovered some of the most valuable aspects of my personality. Without the heartbreak, I may have never found them.

As I resurrect these emotions now, I do so in hopes that what I share may help you to find something hidden inside yourselves. When we have the ability to name our emotions we give them grace. We honor the inner space that they occupy thus freeing the emotion from the prison we keep it in. I believe that feeling is one of our greatest gifts. They are the bridge to wisdom.

There is hope after darkness. Even because of it.

shelby l. lalonde

THE POET

I was born poet.

A hopeless romantic.

An overwhelmed,

intellectual empathic.

Meant to attract the tragic.

Like a magnet I collect their cost.

Sent to unburden the path of the lost.

LOVELESS

There is danger in love stories.

A grasp that won't let up.

A squeeze to your heart that itches ever so fiercely under your skin.

Dancing you to places where sunshine can be a dangerous glory.

There are all kinds of love in this world.

At every turn you must discern its place within your life.

Love has the power to conjure up the deepest forces.

For better or worse.

This is the journey of fools.

And we all are.

So live and let love or be loveless.

You always have a choice.

shelby l. lalonde

SCRATCHING I

He was an escape for her,

the perfect distraction from who she really was.

REDNECK FUCK

I feel like one of those women in your country songs.

Waiting up for you all night long.

Waiting for you to be back where you say you belong.

I'm walked all over,

and I take you back.

It's your fabricated little lovers trap.

Unsatisfied you are by your foolish actions,

dumbfounded you are by my reactions,

the games you play where your guilt can go,

to stick to your egos ebb and flow.

I'm offended and just damned disrespected.

While I walk here in your dreams,

my head's full of frustration and screams.

shelby l. lalonde

My tears full of rage,

because you can't be swayed.

I feel like a stranger.

Like my heart's a beggar.

You make me feel desperate and disoriented.

Your whirlwinds insane.

It brings me nothing but shame.

So I'm gonna go find love and make it bury you.

Because you'll never feel more love than I gave

you but you don't know that now.

SCARLET LETTER

Your morbid interpretation of love has been embedded into my soul.

It was easier than the thought to let you go.

I never thought for a moment that you might have the gall,

the imagination,

or capability to do what you did to me.

As if I were your scarlet letter.

A burden you carried.

You forced me out then wouldn't let go.

I'm so tired of your hatred,

so crushed by your grief.

I gave you everything,

and you gave me nothing but deceit.

shelby l. lalonde

I like the truth entirely too much to exist here with you.

Being evicted from your life so incomplete.

Then back again with the stomp of your feet.

What makes me so negotiable?

I guess my heart can be sacrificed.

Some people are content with being dissatisfied.

Well I'm not one of them.

It's an enduring adventure you present to me,

but you manipulate to keep what you could never really have.

You can't even touch it,

taste it,

or even see it.

So your rage becomes you.

I am truly surprised at my ability to surpass all I believe to be with you.

when love cracks

SCRATCHING II

I was deserted in your darkness.

Always digging my way back out.

Clawing through the creatures you created such
as doubt.

Falling back into them,

every time I said I'd be with you again.

shelby l. lalonde

ABSOLUTION

The thoughts always ticking,

keeping me wishing,

praying for your honesty.

I'm always hopeful,

held up a noble,

even though I hold past memories.

I am aware that hope is a fools remedy,

but loving you is all I see.

I can only deem you worthy now.

And that out of betrayals,

our love be absolved.

DIS-EASE

Recognize that I have tried to compromise.

Nothing's established,

and nothings confined.

Everything you say blows my fucking mind.

Captivated by principles,

singling out tears,

I am a fool discerning what you feed.

Sucking my love with your selfish needs.

All night long inside my head,

I think to leave.

Because tears are worthless here,

and the pain doesn't leave.

It's a cut that gets deeper and I'm bleeding seas.

My heart fucks with my head,

12
shelby l. lalonde

its God damned dis-ease.

I should remember what was beautiful about just
letting go.

Say goodbye and set you free.

I would smile more.

SCRATCHING III

This will make me a better person.

A more interesting artist,

a good counselor.

A compassionate listener,

a more gifted healer,

a better,

stronger version of myself.

This is how I justified it all.

I wasn't wrong though.

shelby l. lalonde

TRIP

Don't try laying that guilt trip shit on me.

Or try to trick me into thinking it's my fault.

It doesn't work with me.

But you can't see that.

You're so unresolved.

Issues beyond what you're capable of
comprehending.

You can't see my worth.

You don't want to.

You only want for yourself.

You're disabled by being unfair.

What a pity.

It's not my fault or even my problem.

Your life is yours.

It's what you've made of it.

So don't make it out to be my fault.

You can't wreck me.

Your unable.

You disgust me with trying.

I'm unsatisfied by simplicity.

I need someone to want to understand my
complexity.

Your unfed mind annoys me.

If you're lazy don't bother me.

If you can't strive for the better good of all,

just walk out my door.

You insult my intelligence and embarrass yourself.

You're naïve to me and worse to you,

to think you can sway,

and repel the truth.

shelby l. lalonde

FOR THE BEST

I don't ask the questions anymore,

because then there's no opportunity for them to lie.

I'll just say okay,

I'll see you when I see you.

I don't attempt to bring them to me because it seems
to have the opposite effect.

Whether indirectly or direct.

I'll just say I love you and hope for the best.

I am myself and I understand that is all I have.

I'll live my life and let them live theirs.

You cannot trap or quarralate.

It makes no sense to dominate.

For all my loneliness,

I am anyway.

So what does it matter to fight or deny,

it's the same in the end,

and no one knows why.

I'll capture what I can again and again,

remember the love that I feel for them.

I'll keep my pain because it is mine.

No one should harbor or be held by my willpower.

Human hatred and how great it is.

I'll remember myself.

I cannot forget,

nor can I neglect,

what I see when I self-reflect.

shelby l. lalonde

MOTIONLESS

Today I was inspired by your delicate kisses.

Your sentimental wishes.

The gift you give,

when you choose it to be given.

Paralyzed in pleasure,

I'm kept from drifting.

An immaculate shift this is from yesterday.

What will tomorrow bring?

Only now I am kept,

and I know all too well it's only for this moment.

But the moment's matter and make my memory.

My memory makes me along with my choices.

And for all I choose I couldn't guess what's next.

It's so uncertain here.

In all your scattered choices.

Unfocused,

unwilling,

swirling souls full of thoughts with no motion.

Killing what we have.

From where we began nothing seems sacred and alive.

Always pain and with that brings me shame.

But another moment I'm bound to create.

My tracks are tailed and I am irate.

Trapped here within your fate.

I'm lingering in the abyss of all of this.

My recognition is my freedom from this instability that I am breathing.

But for now,

I remain motionless.

shelby l. lalonde

CREATURE

If I created you a creature then what did I miss?

Did I unleash something of unmeasured fury?

Is there a consequence I haven't yet discovered?

MORTIFIED

I become more mortified with every hour that this decision lingers within.

My indecision frightens me,

keeps me still,

drowning in unfocused will.

It controls me,

and I can't escape its questions.

It won't let me.

It's dismantling my structure.

Forcing my reflection.

Surrounds me like cement walls.

It's craziness and chaos.

I wish it to stop.

To discover an answer.

22
shelby l. lalonde

The one that I fear.

The one that's waiting,

the one that I hear.

I can't distance myself from it anymore.

It's closing in,

It's drawing near.

It doesn't disappear.

It won't let me ignore,

the fact that I can't do this anymore.

WHEN LOVE CRACKED

She had always lived in the light.

Always.

Protected by some magical force.

The darkness was no stranger to her.

Yet it was completely unable to penetrate her soul.

Something always saved her you know.

So where was the crack?

How did the darkness get in?

Was it the crack in her heart that caused her to
bleed harsh negativities?

Was it because of all her grief?

Is that how it took her over?

Maybe she wanted it to.

shelby l. lalonde

Could it be true that she knew what this type of love could do?

Love cracked.

Will she ever come back from that?

ME

I am myself,

that is all I can be.

I cannot be what you ask of me.

If I were to be,

to do all you ask,

I wouldn't be me at all you see.

I'd be just a pawn in your reality.

Who I am would not be.

We'd both be living miserably.

I came here to live my life as myself.

Why won't you see the value in me?

I have so much to offer.

Something to share.

Why can't you care?

26
shelby l. lalonde

I cannot do what you ask of me.

I can only be myself.

when love cracks

SCRATCHING IV

Love should never remove you from the equation.

shelby l. lalonde

BLUFF

I am overcome with sadness.

The loss of our love deletes my soul momentarily.

Though my hearts sent spinning with the love I feel for you,

I have to let you go.

I've honestly tried living with all your lies,

and all those nights I've sat up to cry.

Your madness is so unfair.

What once was beautiful about you I can't even care.

I'm not so angry this time.

It's just that enough is enough.

I'm calling your bluff.

REFUGEE

When you get sick of the darkness again,

and I'm the only light you see,

baby please,

don't come crying for me.

I know you're just a refugee.

Baby I'll turn you away,

cuz it's the only solace I have.

And I'll cry the tears I can't hold back,

and I'll swim deeper into this heartbreak sea,

cuz I can't escape the hurt you place on me.

You promised the truth and you gave me more lies,

I can't fight out what you still choose to deny.

I guess this is the way that it had to be.

When you love someone as much as me.

30
shelby l. lalonde

It has to be me in the end who would really leave.

This is why your love's no good.

Don't tell me you will do what you think you should.

Tell me you'll do anything and then turn your back
and run,

tell me you can't face me now,

because of what I have become.

It's all in what you have done.

Don't tell me I have a part of your soul and turn
away as I watch you go.

You should've seen the good in grace.

Because what you've done you cannot erase.

So go then baby,

Leave this place.

Cuz the truth for you is too hard to face.

So go then baby,

Now stay away.

Don't make me replay what I can't really ever have anyway.

shelby l. lalonde

SCRATCHING V

Love is a pain we endure in its fragile times.

A feeling unconquered,

with no definable line.

A disguise for something greater within ourselves.

Something that's just outside our reach.

This is what love does teach.

ELUSIVE

It's the eluding the distance between two people that
frightens me.

The distractions that it causes.

So close yet still so far.

So emerged into the other,

yet still so self-involved.

There is no gentle way past this tone,

and I wonder to all relationships is this prone.

shelby l. lalonde

DEMONS

Every vision in my head is clouded with your face.

Been dancing with demons of our love,

cuz it was gone without a trace.

Been trying to sleep,

but I'm up all night with feelings I can't negotiate.

I'm so far gone and I can't go back.

It's like a God-damn heart attack.

Hurts so bad,

and I'm always sad,

I can't wash away your memory.

I'm filtering through all of these thoughts of you,

to place them somewhere,

to set them aside somewhere within my mind,

so I don't have to see them.

But how the hell do you pack up a demon?

THE OWNED

Ever met that one person that your soul seems to crave?

As if you're moved by some imaginary strings that they seem to control.

As if your free will has been overthrown.

Any choice you have had or will have has been taken from you.

Your life is not your own.

You become the owned.

You know better and yet this pulling of strings is so strong it becomes who you are and what you live.

You become so embedded,

cursed within the person's desires that they are your goal now.

It's like watching yourself slip away and ever so slowly you fade.

36
shelby l. lalonde

SCRATCHING VI

It was just four months in,

and I warned myself.

I said,

Get ready,

it's likely I'll be playing ghost for a while.

A conscious transfer from the whole to the hide.

I said stop that now,

it's for me to decide.

Then the Angels came and warned me in my
dreams.

They said,

Your eyes aren't open.

I could see the change within myself,

and so did everyone else.

But I had cleverly written it out.

WICKED

You're supposed to be my friend.

Lift me up when I can't fly,

be my sunshine when I am shy.

In this darkness there is no bliss.

Can't you see what you're creating in me?

I don't know what to do.

Maybe the end of you and me.

It's a distant disaster,

but it's there.

And it's coming for me with wicked flare.

I can't even care.

I've given all I can.

I'll have to let go so that I can live again.

shelby l. lalonde

THE RAIN

I cannot hide the rain within my soul.

It's all because of you,

you know.

I've cried so long for you.

Been torn between what else and what's left to do.

I've given it all away to you.

But you can't see,

in its shamed avenged inability.

Loving you held all my keys.

I'm so happy now to see you leave.

I've collected back to myself all my dreams.

And everything I've allowed you to take from me.

I'm returning to myself.

My dungeon is gone.

And so is your vapid soul.

You were a cipher is all.

And though it hurts,

I can now fill myself back up with my own self-worth.

FADED

What once was beautiful and seemed to glow,

now looks shriveled and is growing old.

This distorted vision you now see every day.

Your growing cold.

You're feeling mislead.

Common thoughts float through your head.

Your complete numb self has swallowed you.

Wasting away is your wisdom found,

your words somehow seem less profound.

Your spirit lies gracefully dormant inside,

the kingdom you cleverly choose to hide.

Encased by your hate,

so consumed with regret,

you yourself,

your greatest threat.

Punishing yourself for what you think you lost,

and all you believe that it has cost.

Can you see the error in your ways?

Envision times of greater days?

Can't you see the part that all of this plays?

Gain some wisdom from your discerning self?

See yourself with forgiving eyes?

Love your darkness as well as your light.

Understand them both to see the truth.

Isn't that what you wanted most?

Have you failed?

Do you really think?

Be as open to yourself to others.

I am asking you only to discover,

that in loving all aspects of yourself,

you will recover.

shelby l. lalonde

THE SHADOW ONE

The shadow one has taken me.

Swallowed me and hidden me.

Corrupted and molested me.

I am small now.

I can barely feel who I am.

My breath has faded and I am weak.

I am almost nonexistent.

And shrinking smaller I do fear.

It's dark here.

And gloomy.

My own death surrounds me.

I'm fading.

I'm wasting away.

My efforts to grow do not escape this place.

My will is weak and so small is my light,

I have no strength left in me to fight.

There's nothing here to save me this time.

To die this death seems my only choice.

I am numb,

and sleeping again.

I do not remember who I am.

An unconscious corpse.

The worthless.

I am the walking dead.

shelby l. lalonde

ANGER

My anger resides here.

It is with me now.

My body never tenser,

my words never more cruel.

I tried to warn you,

I knew it was coming.

I don't know its boundaries,

I can't feel its frame.

It's constantly running through my every vein.

I wish for its seizing,

to make it go away,

but I have to feel it,

so that I may be free again.

I'm sorry to all who come face to face with my rage.

Please remember my love and that this is just a phase.

shelby l. lalonde

FLIGHT

I was flying across an ocean of almighty emotion,

in which I was swallowed,

Completely drowned.

The bird in me longed to resolve this.

To bring me safely to steady ground.

But I was deep,

to far down.

Still something inside me remains unfound.

SCRATCHING VII

Here it is.

My general admission.

My front row seat to my Paramount
Pictures masquerades.

Why do I keep playing these games?

shelby l. lalonde

SNOW

The beauty of the snow falling into the light is the
beauty I wish to be.

To shine and sparkle up above as I come to lay
peacefully on the ground.

The intense quiet of my white blanket,

the vision so perfect,

so unflawed.

I wish I could be that beautiful.

ICE

The harsh temperatures in this reign have kept me ice cold.

I'm stuck here in this beauty filled snow.

I want to grow,

but this winter,

you know.

I was born of us.

My heartbeat slowed,

our relationship has plagued me this.

It's human error I cannot dismiss.

I bare the sorrow now.

shelby l. lalonde

But I do not break.

Not for another man shall my heart shake.

I will not allow myself again this mistake.

No man will break through,

Perfection is now my dignified truth.

I'm aloof.

No sensual concerns,

nothing any longer that my deep heart yearns.

ICE QUEEN

...is the ice queen when I hurt the most.

Searching the darkness for the holy ghost.

An angelic being...

Or human host.

shelby l. lalonde

UNKEPT

This place is a wreak.

So unkept.

It's like the mirror image of my heart.

I became the ice queen so as to protect what's left.

But it hasn't helped me yet.

So I'm picking away at it as I sit here with regret.

Living half alive,

chasing down your lies,

with no one to blame but myself.

No one to save me from this mess.

At least I'm feeling something now.

Better than nothing at all.

SCRATCHING VIII

No storm nor darkness lasts forever,

be courageous and weather what must be
weathered,

keep the light in view.

Keep true,

and nothing can be hidden from you.

shelby l. lalonde

WILLINGLY

You've gone back again from where you came,

I've only myself to blame.

I listen to your lies,

willingly,

I veil my eyes.

Consecrate myself within the sin you choose to live in.

Because I still want you.

Even though it's me that you kill.

And all the dreams you don't fulfill.

I'm reaching out to you now,

with no answer at all.

So I guess there's nothing left.

Just to accept.

Because I still exist only in fragments without you.

PARALYZED

Tempted I am in either direction,

I'm floating here in emptiness.

This vacancy it keeps me still.

Paralyzed yet again by my lover's eyes.

Those beautiful words you've used to disguise,

who you truly are inside.

shelby l. lalonde

OFFENDER

Inspire me you do.

You nutcase offender.

A lawbreaking witness couldn't resist this.

The best of the worst couldn't do you in.

You shame even sinners.

You try to hold back your disgusting disguise,

that despicable juice that pours from your eyes.

But dirty blood runs through your veins.

You've invented all your pain.

Ripped up,

your crazy,

insane.

Your torn by the game.

You abuse yourself but you will not abuse me.

My ego ignites and takes over any pleasure I have of our love.

I hate it.

And I hate that I hate it.

shelby l. lalonde

EXCUSE

You say you can't keep trying to make me love

you.

That's all you do.

But listen,

that's just the excuse for you.

You need someone to blame for why you feel blue.

So you create all these fancy distractions.

And reasons why,

to justify all the fucking lies.

ENOUGH

As if I'm chasing some elusive love song that's not so real.

Why do people say that you will know when enough is enough?

And how do you know when enough is enough?

Especially when you thought before that enough was enough?

I don't know but you just do.

shelby l. lalonde

MORAL

How does one keep their moral graphs intact in
times like these?

With the humming of those who choose to convict
you,

and plummet you to sin.

How is one able to become whole again?

THOUGHTS

Funny how things can change in an instant.

How thoughts occur,

and a reality is shaped.

Can a thought be a mistake?

Is it only the action that one might take?

I always thought it was the action does your
character make.

How your strengths are shaped.

However,

thoughts do create,

and to that there can be no mistake.

shelby l. lalonde

WRINKLE

So love be cherished with all its pain,

wrinkle,

Then cure you,

twisting your veins.

The tempting visions of all that remains.

Its loving projections.

Tender injections.

It's beautiful.

How curious.

All of it.

However painful.

The defeat is so discreet.

It's just that passion be so tempting.

SCRATCHING IX

If a woman shares with you the songs that live in
her soul,

listen to them,

for she's telling you who she is.

shelby l. lalonde

SCRATCHING X

I hide with you here.

I do.

But I know that the reason is not for you.

What am I so afraid of out there away from you?

This is what you've taught me to do.

INJUSTICE

I've sacrificed my identity,

repel the inactivity.

It's creepy to me really.

It's injustice to me.

It signals dirt and vengeance across my soul.

Mad at myself for letting you through,

and finding your way into my weaknesses like you
do.

Your brilliant at creating more.

Gotta face that you're as crafty as me.

Only I lift you up,

as you watch me self-destruct.

shelby l. lalonde

YOUR DEATH

I'm purging up the thoughts of us as if the devil himself burrows inside of me.

As my body tries to free them,

my flesh is burnt beyond an established life planned free.

This wall I can't cross inside of me.

You've created for us misery.

Why can't you see?

I want to be free.

You are no longer meant for me.

I'll have to think you dead to get you out of my fucking head.

My body,

my mind,

You're even taking my spirit.

Can't you hear it?

SECRETS

You walked in weakness.

You kept your secrets.

You wouldn't trust me enough to let you live.

But I did.

You'd forgotten what I'd give.

I can't carry it all sometimes.

But I do it anyway.

It's of no choice to me,

you've made everything so uneasy.

You follow me.

I want you to free me.

My own light's so dim and you don't care.

They gave me a gift,

and I gave it away for you.

68
shelby l. lalonde

Now,

I'm so sorry and sorrowful.

Go just leave.

Please.

But you can't even give me that.

You can't ever leave me alone like that.

Your stuck so deep,

I'm like another little dirty secret that you keep.

SCRATCHING XI

This pen relieves the pressures from within my body when the emotions come.

Them really strong ones.

To write prevents the explosion any people would see.

The unconscious depths of me.

So instead I let it all spew from my pen,

but now to write even just depends.

I bet this is why I no longer like who I am.

shelby l. lalonde

VANITY

Are you still not humbled my darling so vain?

Visions of venture and virtues in brain?

Are you still sitting holy and high?

Your glitter caught by every eye?

Are you still not fearful?

Still center is self?

While all you love seem to fade and melt?

Are you still clueless?

And unpretentious?

I can see where you are headed.

Someday you'll see what you've neglected.

When I'm not there and no one cares.

When you're all alone and you are scared.

Like the many times you've done that to me,

gripping and pleading for my sanity.

Someday you will pay for your vanity.

shelby l. lalonde

SCRATCHING XII

You've opened doors inaccessible by others.

PAPER

Resting in your castle here with all my paper

wishes I have blistered feet.

Where's my defeat?

My search is barren.

Raw.

My fortune still sits within,

even with my second sight.

So I'll draw them out still as scribbles from my pen.

Knowing one day,

I'll make sense of where I've been.

Be able to see the purpose and the gifts of all of

this.

shelby l. lalonde

SCRATCHING XIII

I can't fight tonight.

Sometimes it just all falls into a deep dark midnight.

I'm lost to devils here.

Surrounded by demons.

Bound to a hell I can't dispel.

This is what my story tells.

These are the makings of my madness.

WATERFALL

Maybe it's the weather?

Or some sentimental notion to capture your attention.

Maybe it's some form of emotional dehydration,

where I'm in need of some vast flood or just an innocent gesture.

For a trace of the grace I felt when we'd walk down a path.

Something just within my grasp.

It all happened so fast.

Not intended to last I suppose.

I'm left with elements and fractions.

I can't subtract them in any equation.

It happened.

A couple of words can change everything.

76
shelby l. lalonde

It wasn't the words let's get that right.

It was way before the words.

The teeter tottering of suggestions from habits
granted unclear.

Weighted by a world of creation that neither you nor
I could escape.

We are all artists here.

But we create landscapes much vaster than the
cleverest of passer byers.

Awakening the delicate and untouched.

Wanted or wicked.

No one's left unchanged.

Sure,

I'm still navigating through the crowd.

I see you.

The waterfall within me spoken.

SCRATCHING XIV

When love cracks you open,

journey deep inside.

shelby l. lalonde

HONEST LISA

If I can be honest with you for just one moment,

if I were to tell you all I've done,

if you knew who I really was,

could you still love me with all my hatred?

My manipulations and all my judgments?

My feelings of demand?

When I am dirty,

gritty with greed,

emotionally sinking and in your need?

Do you think our relationship would succeed?

Could you still find what's perfect in all my
imperfections?

Find sanity in when I am insane?

Beauty and when I am vain?

And all I do to ease my pain.

If I were to tell you what a fool is made of you,

Is that something you think we could get

through? If I were to tell you all that's true,

or will it fail as relationships do?

shelby l. lalonde

SCRATCHING XV

I cannot change what I have become.

Only accept what has made me numb.

Our love.

Though *why* is not upon me,

there's a trust in me that I can't deny.

I trust that one day I'll know why.

POETIC

I can't explain the pain.

I have no words for all these tears.

I'm obliviated,

captured now by fears.

Catastrophic is my anger.

And its expression is tears.

Maybe today I'm just not poetic.

With this life being so hectic.

My words are my savior and I need them

now. They've always helped me through

somehow. Look at what I do have.

I should be glad.

Stop being so fucking sad.

My glossary proceeds me.

82
shelby l. lalonde

MIDHEAVEN

He's becoming frustrated with my elusive nature.

I'm not solid.

I can't be.

It's not who I am.

I'm in,

I'm out,

I'm always in between.

I'm in midheaven.

Collecting.

Capturing things that most just can't see.

How can I possibly be what he needs?

Or he me?

LEARNED

You know what I've learned.

I've learned that if you don't know what you've learned then it's not over.

Disturbed by this chapter of your life?

The book that had no ending?

Trying to find some reason within?

Make some sense of an insane thing?

You look so hard,

and then it hits.

It's left unwritten without a script.

It hasn't ended.

You anxiously await its resurrection.

shelby l. lalonde

LOVE

Its mysteries unfound.

Leaves me wrapped here in feelings so profound.

TAPESTRIES

The depths of my love are varying tapestries into
the depths of the deepest of souls.

If you can see into my eyes there will be doorways
you will find,

they open reaching past all time.

Passages to bridges across our universe.

Recognize first,

that this trickles out from within me in simple
pleasures.

Elevating measures.

You may brush its wind,

or feel its waters,

be warmed by its fires,

even grounded by its sands,

if you take into yours my hands.

86
shelby l. lalonde

I keep this protected because it frees.

Do you deserve me?

Do you know the force of what you might find?

What this love shows,

do you really want to know?

Can I trust you with its treasures?

Its varying,

unwavering measures?

What might be the reason for the way I feel about you.

Can you answer this question?

give me clues?

Should I fall this way into you?

Can you keep my kingdom kept?

Not neglect?

Have respect?

Keep the balance of male and female in check?

Control what you want to manifest?

Do you recognize these treasures?

If corruption came,

would you leave it in vain?

Forget what we became?

THE OBSERVATION

Being with him was like being sure I disliked myself.

Keeping me distracted from who I knew I was,

what I could become.

The ultimate form of self-sabotage.

A prevention tactic of my own creation.

What an art.

Such a creatrix.

I crafted this life all my own,

to keep myself from living my fullest potential.

This was the highest form of irresponsibility.

Am I really this lazy?

Or was I really just not ready?

I'd like to go with the latter.

One cannot ever really run from who they know

they are.

it's always there,

waiting for you,

follows you like a ghost,

adventuring alongside its human host.

Whispers to you.

Reminders that you are forced to notice.

Not allowing you to give up.

Keeping you conscious.

Waking you up.

SCRATCHING XVI

It isn't hard for me because I don't understand,

it's hard for me because I do.

OVERRATED

Wider awake than I've been in a while,

I'm finally starting to fucking smile.

I can see the chaos I once created,

I'm trying to say that love was *overrated*.

My herringbone dreams are all out the window.

It's okay though,

I see what's important.

Knowing myself,

being open.

I must salvage what I am proud of.

Because all I thought,

was an illusion.

shelby l. lalonde

TRIGGER

Clear as a picture and just like that,

the words produce a visual map.

Bringing a memory back.

You react.

You never forget words like that.

And anyone who says them,

triggers you back.

Because you'll never forget words like that.

SCRATCHING XVII

Why do I rescue people to the point where I hurt
myself?

AWAKENED QUEEN

Rested in your kingdom of pain,

with nothing to gain

I envy you.

For reasons unknown,

you sit on this throne,

I bow below,

to these visions I'm shown.

Your egos seen for miles beyond my eyes.

Your headstrong denial,

so revealed in your smile.

A false power given to you by me.

In an effort to help you to cope with reality.

Because I am engrossed with lust for your mouth on
my skin.

The way you kiss me,

how you begin.

My God I named you.

From an instilled remembrance of something long past.

A sensation from within my being.

An overwhelming feeling.

You give only pleasure to make yourself feel better.

You know not love.

It's selfishness that keeps me here.

I am no victim.

I am completely aware.

And you look upon me as if I am unenlightened,

unsuspecting to your game.

But I'm playing with a fire that I've ignited.

It's only extinguish,

is to leave all of this.

shelby l. lalonde

Control is a trait that I'd rather need of myself for myself.

Not be deemed by you.

You are a fool on an immature rampage.

And I play along.

To bring you wisdom,

to one day leave you lonely in your kingdom.

To show you what it is that you instill,

and also what you kill.

Sadly,

what you gave me.

DUPLICATE

I know that you use my words because you lack the courage to form your own.

You mimic me,

because you yourself do not know how to be.

From inside yourself you cannot see anything to be worthy.

So you re-create what's outside yourself.

You,

yourself,

you do not know.

So you follow.

CAN'T

I can't keep the passion without the adventure.

I can't have structure without the truth.

I can't feel happy without the openness.

I can't be open without the love.

And without the truth,

there is no love.

DEVIL

My devil still knocks at 4 AM,

wants me still to let him in,

but I can't take his hand.

He still wants to play in the city of the damned.

A DIMENSION OF LOVE

Love is like a river with the currents undefined,

causing much deep and inner twine.

Where in love does one draw the line?

With memories of love triumphant in the mind.

The twisting and turning,

the feeling of being in and of the divine.

Are you like me?

Do you fight with this reality?

Challenges of heart ripping your inner apart?

<u>ONCE</u>

Once upon a time there were flowers,

sunshine,

and plenty of time.

Or so it seemed.

Then it came upon me,

a time for sadness.

There were no more greens or rays of light,

only darkness and not only at night.

It was supposed to happen,

fate you see,

it was the end of you and me.

It was just meant to be,

to all fall apart.

Of the time it took to mend my heart.

102
shelby l. lalonde

It seemed my soul had been torn apart.

Finally,

you see it all came to me.

The rules of the earth,

and of this plain,

it was on that for my soul to claim.

And you know it never goes,

that pain,

but wisdom seems to be what I have gained.

In the loss of you I found some strength.

I thank you for this piece of me,

it will now forever be with me.

And this is why I think you see,

that you and I were meant to be.

MY SLEEPING LOVER

Mysteriously dark,

yet shiny and true.

Never giving up what you feel to do.

A place of warmth,

and comfort to,

yet held back courage lingers and you.

The beauty of your eyes,

yet in disguise.

My sleeping lover,

do you see me to?

shelby l. lalonde

ODD THINGS

There are very odd things and they don't go.

Funny,

I'm a very odd thing and I don't go.

Funny when odd things go.

We know we miss them though.

BECAUSE

Because Loveless is a failure.

An exposed lie of an internal truth.

Fight-less-ly naming movements I barely can take.

Because my name is a fraud.

It's backwards is as backwards does.

In truth it should be love as it always was.

Because my own laughter pulses my body in
shockwaves,

the rubber buffer between the waking dream and
the reality seen.

Because the dialogue is being spelled out on the
walls like I'm watching a drive-in picture screen,

a scripted paradox of the lives I've lived.

Because his whispers in the wake so vivid as my
body shakes, makes the only moments I'm really
alive.

106
shelby l. lalonde

I thrive within the shape of his eyes.

Because my wicker heart burns away there,

leaving an internal darkness I crawl through
daily.

Because written in the pages of my journals voice,

are the consequences of living this waking hell,

here,

where I do not really dwell.

Because the only thing spinning is me and I can
barely breathe in the circles of his 3-D reality.

Because I feel red textured,

pain and I valley through the

hurt.

Because the exits wrapped in hard leather been

corrupted by cloudy weather.

Because he's shaking my brains most.

Because hidden within it is my ghost.

DEEPLY

If life is supposed to be so dark,

then make it not so.

I want to be cradled from my head to my toes.

No more disaster,

I keep running.

Spinning faster.

Let me be loved beyond compare.

I ask for the one that knows,

be known.

Enable my freedom and destinies care,

no longer let love end in despair.

Let me offer what I can give.

I promise I'll never let his heartache live.

Not a care in the world,

shelby l. lalonde

love should be.

I know this is what's meant for me.

Bring him to me.

There couldn't be a creature that would love him
more deeply.

FATHER

Father what do you see when you look at me?

Father why do you crucify me?

What have I done but only love?

When my heart is filled with courage,

you fill with rage for my standing tall.

Disgusted you seem to have me in your sight.

What is it in you that I ignite?

Is it her you see?

My mother you hate?

Or maybe simply your own reflection?

Father tell me what have I done?

What do I do?

Do I inhibit you?

Make you feel things you'd rather avoid?

shelby l. lalonde

Do I make you squirm or feel paranoid?

Embrace me father what do you fear?

I am your child,

your daughter dear.

Father look at me.

Comprehend what you see.

The truth of it all,

what is me.

I burn in your fire father.

I am your creation.

The heaven in you has been born into me.

I hold your dignity.

I cherish you,

I need you to be captured for a moment by what you
see.

All I ask father,

is that you recognize me.

SCRATCHING XVIII

Violent pain crashes my forces,

making me weep at what my life's course is.

Feeling never so stronger than I am now.

But hungry for love,

a better life somehow.

shelby l. lalonde

SCRATCHING XIX

I've stolen back from that thief.

The manipulations,

the hurt.

I laugh inside now.

Hurt became the concrete base to face what I never
thought I could.

Where pain had muddled my laughter,

I could never have guessed what came after.

SCRATCHING XX

And there you have it.

The seriousness of this risk.

I risk myself.

My heart.

Being utterly torn apart.

Every levy eventually breaks.

Catastrophe in its wake.

How built upon is your hearts foundation?

How stable is your inner creation?

THE HEARTBREAKING FOG OF ALCOHOL

I'm keeping myself in this heartbreak fog.

I won't let myself out,

I won't dare.

I won't be found.

I can't admit.

I still have pain that I can't fix.

I still deny.

Choosing to hide it from everyone's eyes.

It's stuck in my throat because I won't speak it.

I hold it there like it's a secret.

I'm judging it as weakness.

This downward dagger still piercing my heart.

It's cold and shameless,

brittle and dark,

but I don't dare to tear myself apart.

I can't surrender to it,

or explore,

so I'll keep pretending that I don't care to know myself anymore.

I can't face it.

Can't lay my fingers around it to trace it.

You didn't only break my heart you broke my spirit.

And I'm still mad.

I've taken the madness to a whole other level.

That's why I've named you my devil.

I suffer every day.

Just now,

today,

in different ways.

Ones of which I could never say.

shelby l. lalonde

The hardest thing I've ever done was walk away.

I don't know which is better.

Apart or when we were together.

I don't want to look at the pieces you took.

I won't even write about it in my stupid little book.

So I just promise to keep breaking my own heart.

I choose to stay heavy.

Where I can make sure that tomorrow is the same.

Where I've fallen deeply into the mundane.

A deliberate reoccurrence of similar days.

Where I'm held hostage by time in this alcoholic
haze.

Keeping myself from my uncomfortable fortune.

EMBERS

Lost within the embers of my mind there are lost fragments of who I am.

My hearts too tender and I don't remember where I placed them.

I seem so hidden,

totally unforgiven.

In everything I do this shows.

I am nothing now but ashes you know.

shelby l. lalonde

SCRATCHING XXI

Being broken has always been part of the plan.

FOOL

Never loveless again?

Is this a joke?

Are you a human hoax?

Surely you've never met a holy ghost.

Do you even know what you just said?

Well,

let me explain something to your head.

You can't even fathom the depths of my heart.

What I wake with on a daily basis.

What I carry in my graces or know that I've covered
all my basis.

Your love,

I'd never disrespect.

You're an arrogant fool and kind-of cruel.

Though you look like a peace-loving hippie-

And I know in your way,

You're doing your part.

But back off what your visually flawed perception of non-depth never had any part.

No understanding of.

You have no idea the kindling you just lay.

Or the symphony of chaos coming your way.

You think you can measure my love?

Act as though your jury or judge?

You don't know me.

And that I loved his authenticity.

His genuine incapability.

He's a master disaster.

A charged-up force field creating fires that burn bones.

Cores souls.

That's I bet something you didn't know.

ALOOF

A certain amount of aloofness seems to be a
requirement in life.

A survival tactic of which can have many
advantages.

PANDORA'S BOX

She felt the weight of all her worlds.

All its evils on her shoulders.

For evil loves free will.

And the destructive properties of its curiosities.

Preys on the human traps of its ego you know.

In its weak moments,

evil can find you.

Your darkest self.

Because you have one.

We all do.

Evil is patient.

Evil is virtuous too.

Balance is heaven.

And so is hell.

So we remain wrapped in human paradox.

Our personal Pandora's box.

As we try to configure pieces of our reality together,

strategically knowing it doesn't really matter.

Because it's all okay whatever we choose.

With Pandora's box we have nothing to lose.

shelby l. lalonde

THE PROPHECY

My angels turn as I fall to the ground,

sinking deeply,

without a sound.

Hearing my echo,

holding me still,

praying for me to use my will.

Knowing what one day I could fulfill.

TIME TRANSCENDS

Time bends.

It flexes in our favor.

It can reach back and change our perception.

Cascades over our past events.

Trades emotions,

loosely invents.

It's all a matter of your resistance,

or persistence.

The emotional connection of what's true for you,

it's always changing.

Time delves deeply into the caverns of our
existence.

It measures perspective.

Creates space between the original version and its
current tangibility.

126
shelby l. lalonde

Leaves before you the magic to change it.

It crafts the past into a new reality every time you remember it.

Time transcends,

this is true.

It does so with every thought you have,

of the future and the past too.

FRAGILE

I captured myself so graceful that day.

I was sitting in the corner of the bar.

Like I was watching from afar.

I felt my scars.

My hands slithered upside and down them.

The textures have changed in various ways,

sensitive spots,

where the skin is thicker.

Damaged,

like haggard old mascara.

While I kept the tears from drizzling out my eyes,

I felt an envy ignited for myself.

The triggered sadness produced some rapture.

Something I've long wanted to capture.

128
shelby l. lalonde

BALANCE

The capable stars are now lifting you from the
unkept balance within my world.

Disconnecting the cords of the angelic trace of you
that was hence displayed with indignity.

Though I'll always love you anyway,

The chains are now broken.

My balance has been restored.

DREAMS

You just keep visiting me in my dreams.

I wake up crying,

I still grieve,

because you just won't leave.

You're a micro magician,

that's a given.

You keep your knowledge,

feelings and wisdom hidden.

You know in this world that you're always forgiven.

You had a good teacher didn't you.

Good thing I know your next moves before you do.

Please leave me alone because it's troubling me.

I did my best for you when we were together.

I promise to always love you I do and I will forever.

130
shelby l. lalonde

WORDS

Your words battered my warmth and captured my strength.

All I forsake.

But I withstood the catastrophic avalanche of all I was.

My death I did not become,

chosen to be the wounded one.

And fighting yes,

that's what you wanted.

You wanted me to bear witness to the darkness.

I did.

I've grasped their insecurities and I made them my own.

And your wavering reality,

your sphere of nonexistence,

as pathetic as it feels,

I can see the stream of beauty flickering throughout this darkness.

All your actions never destroyed divinity.

Yours,

nor mine.

That which you are still exists.

Be unkind to me.

I'm going to care anyway.

I remember now who you are.

You can't make me hate.

Thank you for re-teaching me the truth of what you do.

The darkness is still divinity,

and you're always with me.

shelby l. lalonde

THE UNCOMFORTABLE FORTUNE

It didn't only break my heart it broke my spirit.

Like the fallen tower,

I crumbled to the ground.

Looking for pieces that no longer could be found.

Surrounded by fragments of who I used to be,

intangible traces of what once was me.

The ghosts of persons I've long set free.

Here,

where I met all aspects of my personalities,

in this long-awaited emotional catastrophe.

I began its biopsy.

As the observer of my inner space,

I found this calm that circles me.

There is no fear here.

Nothing to lose.

No expectations about what I should choose.

I've already lost everything within the rubble.

Underneath this darkness that has had me trapped.

I discover the pieces I can't retrieve,

the ones that no longer belong to me.

No longer a representation of me.

It's liberating really.

What I see is my uncomfortable fortune waiting for
me.

The one I buried deep.

What I thought I didn't keep.

All this darkness has shed it to light.

All I see is light.

I can put myself back together now.

Any way that I see fit.

shelby l. lalonde

I suddenly realize,

I could have always done this.

Mold myself carefully into my most cherished
shapes,

Attach my essence,

before it escapes.

MUSEUM

I'm living in my own museum.

My own particular kind of colosseum.

I'm surrounded by,

my core beliefs,

right here,

at home,

where I retreat.

Of course there was a devil in my story.

I keep replying my favorite mythologies.

HAUNTED

What do you see when you look at me?

Am I your ever-loving fleeting dream?

Your gentle queen,

maybe something in between.

Are you enchanted?

Mystified maybe?

Why is it that your still haunting all my worlds?

HIM

He is the other half of her.

He is black and she is white.

He knows who he is,

what he wants,

and how to get it.

He understands what he does.

He knows why and who he is.

He is conscious of himself.

He knows his body just the same.

He knows why he moves the way he does and for
what purpose.

It's beautiful to him.

He loves himself.

For these reasons he knows you to.

138
shelby l. lalonde

For these reasons he also loves you.

He is capable of knowing others before they know
themselves.

He does not judge,

he is open and ego free.

And he wants you to be.

He sees beauty in everything.

But because he is black he can also see your darkest
parts.

The ones even you fear exist,

and may not even know do.

He can even bring them out in you.

He wants you to feel them to know they are there,

he wants you brave,

strong and aware.

He is capable of moving through many worlds.

He knows they exist he denies them not.

He is waiting for her to journey with him.

To make it finally to their solemn kingdom.

Perfect lovers in their one body.

Perfectly same yet opposite to.

She is white.

She knows what he knows and can do the same
things.

But her message is love and the light she brings.

She'll lead you to feel so you can finally heal.

She will help you to find the compassion you can
have for yourself.

They are at the same level of consciousness.
Though right now apart helping the world change
and grow.

Until the time we all end the game, let it go.

For now they wait and watch for their beloved.

They can hear each other's whispers through the

shelby l. lalonde

winds of change.

They are so close yet still so far.

They speak to each other,

their hearts can hear.

One day they will hold each other again.

They need each other that is all.

The way it was before the fall.

SCRATCHING XXII

The dreams continue to haunt me,

And this is what it taught me.

shelby l. lalonde

About the Author

Shelby L. LaLonde is a Strawberry Blonde Gemini mystic who loves all things metaphysical. She gardens, loves to dance, and though many know her as a photographer, she will tell you that her "true love is to write." Shelby is a Certified Psychic and Reiki practitioner who remains a member of the International Honor Society having studied at Cazenovia College and Syracuse University. She is a member of the CNY Creative Writers Café. She lives in a small village near Syracuse New York with her husband John the Pisces.

Also by Shelby

Hope After Darkness Poetry Collection

Book One: When Love Cracks
Book Two: Her Uncomfortable Fortune
Book Three: Venus Rising

Made in the USA
Middletown, DE
14 May 2019